SWEET CORE ORCHARD

Molly –   12/1/09

I hope to get one of
your best sellers eventually!
keep that focus, and
thank you for coming to
the reading.

                    Ben

SWEET CORE ORCHARD

Poems by

Benjamin S. Grossberg

UNIVERSITY OF TAMPA PRESS • TAMPA, FLORIDA

Cover art: "The Garden of the Hesperides" by Frederic Lord Leighton
© National Museums Liverpool, Lady Lever Art Gallery

Manufactured in the United States of America
Printed on acid-free paper ∞
First Edition

The University of Tampa Press
401 West Kennedy Boulevard
Tampa, FL 33606

ISBN 978-1-59732-053-5 (hbk) • ISBN 978-1-59732-054-2 (pbk)

Browse & order online at
http://utpress.ut.edu

Library of Congress Cataloging-in-Publication Data

Grossberg, Benjamin S. (Benjamin Scott), 1971-
   Sweet core orchard : poems / by Benjamin S. Grossberg. -- 1st ed.
      p. cm.
   ISBN 978-1-59732-053-5 (hbk : alk. paper) -- ISBN 978-1-59732-054-2 (pbk : alk. paper)
   I. Title.
   PS3607.R656S84 2009
   811'.6--dc22   2008053230

Contents 🌿

Had I Been There, Had It Been Me ⚬ 3

🌿

Pig Auction ⚬ 9
Beetle Orgy ⚬ 13
Terro Ant Killer ⚬ 17
Why God Hated Onan ⚬ 20
Incantation ⚬ 24
God on the Treadmill ⚬ 26
The Journey Down ⚬ 28
Asked What He's So Afraid of, He Pauses ⚬ 31
Cocktail Party ⚬ 34

🌿

Childhood Incident ⚬ 39
Blue-Black ⚬ 42
How to Care for an Air Fern ⚬ 45
Time and Place ⚬ 49
Bioluminescence ⚬ 52
Holding Hands ⚬ 54
Like the Back of My Hand ⚬ 56
Adwaitya and the Fruit Fly ⚬ 58
Ambition ⚬ 61

🌿

Two Apples ⚬ 67
The Colossus at Rhodes ⚬ 73
In Memoriam: Ginger ⚬ 77
Purgatory ⚬ 80

Adam's Punishment ⚘ 83

Stark Brothers ⚘ 87

The Trees Arrive ⚘ 90

Not Children ⚘ 94

Greening Song ⚘ 96

Notes ⚘ 101

Acknowledgments ⚘ 103

About the Author ⚘ 107

About the Book ⚘ 109

For Steven R. Young,
who helped me plant the trees

SWEET CORE ORCHARD

Had I Been There, Had It Been Me

Always the script, the dramatic comma,
the pointed ellipsis, half turn, beat, the exit
itself as punctuation. Let's say the back wall
of the house fell away: first cracks
down the plaster, then it crumbles
to reveal seventy-five rows of spectators.
That's the explanation: they've been there
all along; I mulled blocking on a blind
impulse, but it turns out a correct one.
Maybe someone is making love to me
(in the 19th century sense): do I throw off
his hand, exit with pithy wit? Or simply
submit to it: the sappy moment
which will, I know, have to be resisted
in some later scene. Had I been there,
had it been me, I would have said—
and the audience would have been moved
to applaud. Astounding improvisation!
I'd have walked right up to the lawyer,
the bank manager, and I'd have said—
or, if it was me, it would never have gotten
that far; I'd have turned to her and said—

So I am contemplating in its shade
an apple tree. Haven't I often done that?
So why not me? Late August, the leaves
like arrowheads, dark green, waxy,

punctuated by apples—constellations
of apples. There I see The Hunter, bow
pulled back, the apples of his quiver fixed
with perfect aim: William Tell, daughter
across the tree, of apples herself, poised
with a perfect fruit above her head:
wet tension of its surface, red skin
that kisses the sun. And this perfect tree.
This perfect tree in which every stamen
was touched by pollen, in which every
flower thickened to fruit: tree that knows
by its own example perfection. In each
cluster, five apples bunch as tight
as chambers of a human heart. Had I
been there, had it been me—and the slither
up the trunk brought my attention low,
the rippling body sliding along the trunk,
I who have been so good all these years
at resisting, and giving in, and resisting—
I'd have heard the melodious hiss, seen
the glinting tongue, its fork invading
the region of my heart, the archer
in that perfect canopy aiming right at me,
I who have given in to desire
when the stakes were much lower,
could I resist those movements, how fully
the serpent's hiss gives itself over to simile:

I am like, I am like, I am like. . . .
Seen it before, mister. I'd have sighed
in an aside, glanced up at the sky,
deadpanned the audience, and said—

Or had my lover brought the apple.
For years I have told them not to burn
money on me. But to bring only this,
to hold it out with a silent smile
as they enter the house, down center
on the stage of the palm. No better way
to say I love you. So why not me?
Early October, the outsize hunger
after running, and my lover brings it over.
I recognize on his breath the scent
of the serpent, and the apple, the one
forbidden thing. Deep voice, dark eyes,
silent smile and perfect apple;
only midday draped across his body,
tight, alert, alive to the moment of sin.
And reaching out to take it in my hand.
Who better than me? Let the tension
linger, let the audience pulse
with anticipation. We touch over
the forbidden fruit. The stage lights dim,
and I look at him, and I look at him,
and raise my eyebrows, and say—

[5]

But even so, wouldn't I end up here again,
always here? Angels crossing swords
behind me, shame clothing me, conflating
all my losses—the loss of God, the loss
of apples, how they expand inside
to fill up hunger. Maybe there are
no words here, just the sky
blackening with anger. Maybe words
wouldn't be useful here anyway.
Consider a scrim: the night sky blotted
of constellations; nothing but gray
swirls of wrath. And project against it
a man's silhouette: head bent, empty-
handed, the memory of apples imprinted
on his wordless tongue, and around his
neck, loss—like a cowbell—announcing
his presence to the fallen world.

Pig Auction

Three quarter quarter quarter do I have half?
The boy steps aside, and this one, a barrel,
pinkish in the hindquarters and brown
in the fore, trots out in front of the auctioneer
who says a few words—perfunctory, he speaks

much too fast to be understood—before soliciting
bids. The pig meanwhile struts its hour,
walking back and forth below the podium
from which all that sound about it blares.
Struts? No, the pig doesn't strut; the pig in fact

with its curly tail and flat-topped snout
is oblivious to all but the boy, following him
as he circles, waving his yellow pennant
first this way then that in the small pen.
Picture this: a tent, two hundred spectators

on three sides, auctioneer on a dais, his voice
tripping along between speech and song—
and in the dirt pen in front of that dais: pig.
Yes, there are helpers, too: there is the boy
who shepherds the pig; there is a man

in a cowboy hat who points and gestures
at people in the audience, confirming bids—
three seventy-five four four do we have four?

but finally focus is on the pig and its prospects.
From the sidelines where we stand, I suggest

we root for the pig; but you tell me that the pig,
its future in show, breeding, or pork—
most likely a combination—needs no help
in rooting. I turn back to the pen, unconvinced
because the odds seem stacked against it:

the reason? Auctioneer, voice tripping
like water down a rock face. The auctioneer
with his hands raised now, conducting the event
like a symphony. He culminates the audience
to his bidding, pulls the shepherding boy

with his left hand, nods and throws meaningful
glances at the man in the cowboy hat—
maestro conducting with a curly wand.
The auctioneer is the Father, looking coldly
down on the auction of the world that He

creates with an extra-natural fluidity of speech,
incarnates with each trilling syllable
around the sole subject: pig, shepherded back
and forth before spectators it doesn't understand—
does it? Now the shepherding boy and the man

appear as angels, their expressionless faces
enacting bliss. What does that make
the cackling spectators? I become convinced
as we watch—though you are silent, though you
are clearly interested in moving on, in seeing

other things—that with its pink half
and brown half, its cloven hooves, that barely
known to this pig, the auction is an
adversarial relationship. And if so, what hope
for the pig? The auctioneer bangs

his gavel: *sold sold for three seventy-five to.*
From the bench, he sentences pig to the gallows;
the bailiff shepherds it off. Is it mercy,
this pig's ignorance? All the machinery
operating around it, who's to say

the auctioneer isn't a scientist, and the pig
moving back and forth on a glass slide, beneath
an eye larger than the sun? I understand you want
to see cows, sheep, the rows of rabbit cages,
but there will be nothing that we see here

all day, that will be truer than this—
and look, another pig! The auctioneer up there

gets ready to say grace as this pig hustles
onto his dinner plate. This one with red spots,
and now the auctioneer's at it again. . . .

Beetle Orgy

Bloom up from the earth, blooming and curling
like ribbon, and at semi-regular intervals
sprouting leaves: almost the border art
of a Celtic manuscript, the vines up along the fence
of this old tennis court. Amid the wreck

of the net, the cracks of the surface, the rust
along the poles still standing, the vines
are a saving delicacy. Not jarring at all,
though incongruous—except as a reminder
that the school yard will gladly take this place

back in a few untended years, that between
the vines and grass, the tennis courts
will be ground into meal and digested.
I stop at one of the vine edgings caught
by even finer detail: the leaves themselves

are digested; they have been eaten to
irregular lace, and the perpetrators are still here—
five of them across one particular leaf, lined up
straight and even, like cars in a parking lot.
Beetles: their backs a lustrous green and copper,

taken from the kiln hot, thrown on a bed of saw dust
that burst into flame, then lidded over
so the vacuum could draw the metal oxides

to the surface. At first it looks like there are five,
but now I see that there are seven, no eight—

and that in three of the spaces, beetles
are doubled up, one mounting, back legs
twitching as if running and getting nowhere;
and one mounted, also moving, slightly rocking
in back, close to the point of intersection—

or penetration—in any case, where the bodies
touch. And here I come to it—amid the advancing
vines and decrepit court: they're on other leaves, too,
all around—coupling in company, hundreds of them,
the rows melding to make a single metallic band.

Back in Houston, a friend had parties—
lawn bags in the living room numbered with tape
to store guest clothing; plastic drop cloths
spread out in the spare bedroom (cleared of furniture
for the occasion), a tray of lubricants, different

brands in tubes or bottles, labels black, red, and silver
—a high tea sensibility. The artifacts remained
uncollected in his apartment for days, even
weeks after, when I would drop by to find his talk
transformed, suddenly transcendental—

the communality, he told me, the freedom: not
just from the condom code (HIV negative I
was never invited) but freed of individuation—
nothing less than rapture, men more than brothers,
a generosity of giving and taking, to both give

and take greedily, that he had experienced
nowhere else. Could I understand that?
The room pulsing as if inhabited by
a single animal, caught up in a single sensibility.
Could I understand? I could read transformation

in his face, could see his eyes, feel him trying
to tell me something: to offer this reliable revelation—
what he always knew would come, but what always
in coming disarmed him. As he talked I looked around
the spare bedroom, attempting to see it

in terms other than lust—a couple of dozen men,
how they would have lined up, become a single
working unit on clear plastic, how their bodies
might have formed a neat chain. I looked around
and tried; couldn't I understand that?

So each beetle a tiny scarab, a dime-size jewel
that glints in the sun. I lean over and touch
their backs with the tip of my finger: running

up and down the bright, smooth surface
like piano keys, hard enough to feel resistance

but not to interject foreign music. Together they form
a band of light, a band of glaze, the gold leafing
that shadows the vines in Celtic manuscripts, a living art.
Maybe that's how it was at my friend's parties—
God leaning over the house on a casual tour

of the wreck of the world, noticing ornamentation
where it wasn't expected. Moved to add
His touch, He reaches a hand through the clouds, runs
His finger over the hard arch of their backs, covering
the length of each spine with the tip;

each man brightens at the touch, comes to know
something expected, unexpected, and tenuous—
and God, also, comes to some knowledge
as if for the first time, is distracted and pleased
by the collective brightness of human skin. . . .

Then I think of God fitting the roof back on
my friend's house, and exhaling, satisfied—
just like me as I walk away
from the tennis court, just like the men inside.

Terro Ant Killer

All night long: on cardboard squares
the size of my thumb—or slightly larger—

I squeeze the thick syrup. All night long.
A clear drop, like dew rolling off

a morning leaf, as full of light, but thicker,
more viscous. At first only one or two

come. They position their three-part bodies
face toward the pool, and lean in:

all black at the clear liquid. But then
there are more. I count six. I rip off

more cardboard, squeeze more syrup.
I go back fifteen minutes later, and there are

dozens, fifty, eighty. They are crawling
down cupboard walls, coming over

the flour sack like a great hill, over the cornmeal
to their own meal. I rip more cardboard,

fill up the troughs. This goes on.
Soon every trough is circled. Their hard

bodies crawl between, over each other,
their antennae engaged and waving, heads

depressed like those of cows in a field.
I suspend the plastic bottle

over them, and as a drop wells, surges
from the tip, as sweetness bubbles

from the opening, some of them reach up,
rear their forward segments toward the drop,

their front legs churning as if they were horses
about to break into gallop. They lift

their hunger, their fixation. Then the drop
falls and they fall to it, intent

on all physical sweetness. All night long.
This goes on all night. I return

and return; I delight in the progress. I add
more liquid when it is needed

and when it is not. The package
is explicit: they eat, they return

to their nest, they regurgitate, others
eat. They infect each other

in a chain of contact: clever scientist,
I've learned to kill them in just the way

they've learned to live. But the package
does not describe this: rapture, how they

come and come and draw others to come,
how it is an hour, hours later

and their bodies continue to take
and take, how they climb over each other,

bodies intent, focused with a physical
longing I'm sure I've seen

somewhere before. And me, too, I return
and return, all night long. It is hours

for me, too. I'm mired in it. Oh God,
God, tell me it's not really like this.

Why God Hated Onan

"And the thing which he did was evil in the eyes of the LORD. Therefore He killed him also." —Genesis 38:9

1.

Judah's first born, Er, was wicked in the sight of the Lord,
and the Lord killed him. We have no notion of Er's error,
merely that he was "wicked." And as the forms of wickedness
are many, we may picture Er merely dropping
without explanation: Er in the fields, Er with Tamar
discussing the pasture lands of Canaan, Er laid out
on the rushes, Er falling, a stone, behind the team,
Er passing by the side of his brother, Onan.
It must have resembled a heart attack: the same
grabbing of the chest, the fierce look of physical betrayal.
Poor Er: it may be he never knew how he erred.

2.

But of Onan we know—both the act and the issue.
Onan "spilled on the ground, lest he should give seed
to his brother." Onan who must have imagined Tamar's body
his brother's: not Er's property, but him literally,
as if the act of investing her, indeed, would have been
investing him. It may be that there by the fire Onan saw
his brother struck by God; it may be that God's ire
fell over Er like a layer of cellophane, denying his air;
it must be that Onan saw the asphyxiation, his gasping
brother clawing at the neck for breath, unable to say

God does this to me: the hand of God, a choking
hold over my body.

3.

　　　　　　　And there she lay before him: Tamar
in her tent, on her side, naked on clean sheets. Tamar
tawny and nearly hairless, trim Tamar
open to receive Onan as she was bidden to do.
Come to me Onan as your father has commanded us:
raise up seed to your brother, up to your brother
in Heaven, Onan, and into my body, as He
has commanded us. And it must be that he saw
on her body where his brother had lain, and saw also
where he had collapsed
　　　　　　　　　　　out in the fields: running
through the grain as if his robes were on fire, yet
there was no fire; Er who had broken from conversation,
and though there were no flames, who had shot
through the wheat like a meteor, hands over his head,
noiseless screams, his skin blackening and peeling
with the heat of God's disdain; Er collapsing
onto his knees and Onan standing, staring
at his naked wife, whom he was bidden to love.

4.
Onan went in to his brother's wife; he went in
to her. Later, after many years, it must be

that Tamar, too, remembered the moment:
the last time any man had tried to love her,
Tamar dressed in black, mourning two husbands
and denied a third because of how queerly
the first two had died. It must be that Tamar, too,
remembered the instant through a layer of years:
how years can dry a body, how she had been spared
the sight of Er but confronted bodily with Onan,
who pulled out of her—it must have been in disgust—
who overcome

            by something, pulled out of her,
his head filled with images of a body other than hers,
his head filled with images of a body dying
by the awful hand of God; yet whose body quickened
with the physical act, led his hand to drop in an act
of discovery. Onan who remembered God's fist
in the discovery of his own. And it must have been strange
for her: as he backed off the bed, stood before her, his face
a grimace of pleasure and pain, strange for her
as he took vicious grip of his own body, as he spilled
before her on her tent's hard ground.

5.
And in that moment, the Lord: as cross as Olympus
when Prometheus came gripping a brilliant torch. The Lord
His own fist curling in an ire that remembered Er,
His fist forming, a foaming of wrath. And it may be

[22]

that Tamar too was angry. Onan whose knees
struck the hard dirt, as God crumpled him
where he stood, Onan naked in the tent of his brother's wife,
as God compressed the human form in His fist
until He could hear the splinters, the cracking

that indicated human death. And Tamar, perhaps, horrified
and understanding: the years ahead, years unheeded, life
as a widow in their father's house. It may be that she
identified the hand of the Lord, Tamar, that she
conceived of Him His wrath.

Incantation

Goat leggings, Hellenic crags, a cauldron
in the center boiling wine, onions, bay leaf,
the blood of virgins, the blood of whores,
the blood of a few average people, too, like us—
my demonic minions and I are going to dance,
then we're going to spoon the potion
into each other's throats and writhe naked
on the ground, their hooves and claws
making the dirt equivalents of snow angels.
All the while I'll be babbling—Latin, Greek,
Sumerian, tongues I don't know, but still
focusing carefully on your image.
I'll probably have a few relics, too—
a pair of your underwear brewing in the cauldron,
a few toenail clippings in an amulet,
one of your hairs fastened around my thumb.
Do you feel yourself starting to love me already?
I'm fighting a god for you: Jesus, who scowls
at my petty ministrations from a cross,
or who looks down through a well in Heaven
and sees the fire of my cauldron burning
here on Earth. He will have you for church socials,
Easter egg hunts. He is furious when I spend
the night, and you don't get enough sleep
to attend. He will have you for a wife, too,
and grinds his teeth when he guesses
you're in bed with me, snuggling your head

in the hair on my chest. It was for your sake
he added those lines about Sodom and man
lying with mankind; he knew you were
just my kind—and built up his hests
against it. Sometimes Jesus gets the upper hand
and you don't call for a week. Then he gloats,
raises toasts with the Father and Holy Ghost—
three corporate tycoons closing a deal
with champagne. Other times you fold to desire
and they fret. They take out their pocket
watches and look cross at the empty train
platform, before snapping their watches shut.

And now this: me on Earth calling up evil
minions to break you free from your shepherd.
Surely this is too much: in frustration he will
damn us both, which is just what I want.

The truth is, you can keep your god.
I, at least, am willing to share. I'll be satisfied
if you only don the leggings at midnight and dance
until morning. Jesus can have you then, if
he still wants you; you two can frolic on sunlit
hillsides all Sunday. I expect after a day of that
you will again be ready for a little sullying.

God on the Treadmill

Sometimes it takes miles to give up resistance,
though the mirror shows a body unresisting, shows
perhaps something to admire. Others may.
A body without difficulty loosening, breaking
its own willfulness, cracking itself
like a rusted bolt that finally begins to turn.
A body that turns. Toward openness, fantasy,
those desires of and not of the body. Sometimes
I notice a powerful man engaged steadily
repeating difficult action: folding himself, his tight
skin, over and over, lifting a declined torso
or pulling up a suspended trunk, and think,
how neat, how controlled to be inside that body.
I struggle not to stare, grip myself not to lose myself
inside the thought of being inside that body.
I can never get there I know because it is
the image I want, the veneer of muscle
having taken primacy from mind, now first
among equals: bicep, abdominal, quadricep,
the launch after launch of a perpetual run.
I want the image even when I am it, or nearly it—
because even then, I am also that other thing,
self-conscious, burdened, struggling for movement.

If there is a link between God and animals—
the way He identifies with the so much
that isn't us, as He had to have, to have made them—

it must be in the body enacting will immediate
through movement, as if with a word
creating a world (enacting creation immediate
through speech). Which is to say, this is my time
of prayer, my only time: miles in, as long
as it takes for the body to relinquish resistance.
Bright, public, surrounded by others who move
toward better movement. And all the while seeing
in a wall of mirrors that image of myself, deer,
horse, running close kin to breathing, motion
necessary to survival, perfect image of a man
that I'm merely a self-conscious copy of.
I pray for things, of course, for myself
and for those whose pain touches me, selfish
and unselfish prayers for intimates and strangers.
I pray for the runner in the mirror, too, sleek, easy
animal, unselfconscious and present, and absent
as a god, the man who could almost be me,
who I do my best to rush toward. I pray that
one day, by His grace, we may meet.

The Journey Down

Almost mythological. Icarus. The body—
bodies—burned. Dropping from the sky.

But not mythological. The details, physical,
unmitigated by symbolism or allegory.

The twist, or torsion. The ripping. The sound
of impact. The way a body pierces

through a cloud. An entrance wound,
an exit wound trailing wisps of condensation.

How the earth might seem to rise.
The thoughts that might come only

if the eyes were shut. How consciousness already
consumed, or extinguished, or simply gone

off to where consciousness goes, could know
none of it. How the earth would give

for the body on impact. How the crater might
retain the human shape. How this impression

would be mere physics, not love. The descent
of Odysseus, his side padded

by a moleskin of blood, in order to draw
the dead. Learning to get home. The steep

descent of Orpheus, all the while giving
himself to music, his walking feet

a metronome for his grieving heart. And even
Persephone, gagged by a hard black hand

in the back of a carriage. The details
transformed by an explanation of winter:

pomegranate seeds. Six. The blue patch
embossed with the insignia: *Columbia.*

The moleskin, masses of dead giving
way, and Tiresias, the only one still burdened

with memory, steps forward. We place ourselves
among the dead. An arm. A torso.

Identification by a wedding ring. Pictures
on the news. The radio. The pale maiden

crying on the striated shoulder
of the dark God, who tolerates it simply because

he will force her soon. The stories. All
afternoon: the coverage, the people

kneeling to altars in the back of their homes,
journeying to Delphi, where psychedelic gasses

seep up from cracks in the earth—where
the earth gives visions. The people

waiting at the Cape, who fought
their first reaction to radio silence. The event,

even of our moment, lost
already in other headlines. But still

almost mythological. Allegory, symbolism—
blood washes down the throat. Salty. Edged

with iron. A draw no less than that
other solution, the one to which the dead

are urged upon arrival, that makes it easier
to pass the time, that helps them to forget.

Asked What He's So Afraid of, He Pauses

The test. My mother's small, jeweled hand,
nails painted with clear polish. Can I.

Can I write this? The hand
on my chest, and then the sharp

cut of the strap in my shoulder. Then
sound. The test: inevitable. The first time

I heard the word. High school, Annie Clinch
crying in the hall. Someone in class

starts a rumor. *She has it.* The sound
as if from some other event, as abstract

as thunder from lightning. The feel
of my mother's hand, swinging out

from the driver's side. Lurching forward
then back into the seat. Turning

to see the back seat glittering
with glass and unexpected sunlight. *Annie*

has. People denying it merely
to say that word again. *She has.* Annie

in brightly colored Multiples, short
spiky hair, her tears

warm on my neck. Hypodermics
washing up on Sandy Hook. *I should*

hold you. By the bathroom, second bell,
the hall empty except her, squat, hysterical,

shivering. Inevitable: the test
came back. It will be years

before I note the word again. The back seat
littered with diamonds. Sharp lines

of blood down my mother's face,
her lips, from inside

her ear. Her hand clutching
my chest, sign-language letters

above my sternum, my heart. The glint
of rings, glimmer of glass. Suddenly

an intersection: gas stations
on either side of us, faces

appearing in the windows. The sound
of them talking. The test came back—

I can't even write it. "We almost died,"
she says, her palm on my heart, palm

a bracer bar, what they lower
over your shoulders on a roller coaster.

"I don't have it," she says, between
sobs. *What? What is it?* I can't

even write this. The test
came back. The test. See? I can't. I won't.

Cocktail Party

I wouldn't be afraid of dying if there were a mere
four-hour event—drinks, let's say, *hors d'oeuvres*—
at the end of the world. I would arrive early, if possible,
wearing shoes that peg me for the early 1990s
and the nice things I hope they bury me in.
I'd get my drink—vodka soda, lime—grab
a full plate of grapes from the fruit trays, fresh
off those vines still growing
at the end of the world, then begin my rounds.

The first thing of course will be to hear all the news,
to give some and to hear some. The last days
of Pompeii, yes. Maybe I'll tell someone
how the people left cool impressions on the walls.
The Roman Empire? Finite.
I could talk a little about Germanic hordes,
then point a few noble Romans toward better sources.
Someone could tell me how the ice caps fared,
how the American experiment finally turned out,
if the gray wolves made it, if anyone ever read
anything I wrote, what happened
to my brother's children and to my last dog. But

who knows if I'll be able to find anyone
with my personal news. It will be a big room.
I may have to settle for the cosmic: did the Democrats

ever reform healthcare? How did we manage
once fossil fuels ran out? I will not look
for Shakespeare, no doubt at the center
of a large crowd on one of the balconies; I will not
hang out with Karl Rove, alone at one of the bars,
even when I go back to refill my glass. I will also

not be polite if I see anyone I knew but didn't like.
This is the end of the world we're talking about.
I'll have risen from a very long wait in the grave
and no doubt will not be in the mood to have any more
of my time wasted. If I meet a Viking,
I may ask about the journey across the Atlantic
in a long boat. If I happen on my mother,
I'll probably pose my few lingering questions
about the cruelties she inflicted on me in childhood.
But that's it. Mostly I just want to know
that we all made it out together—
if not alive—and that we all can mingle
in one large room, listening to a single four-piece,
sipping really big drinks mixed by the angels.

I guess I just want the assurance right now,
before time goes even one bit further,
that I'll get to come back at the very end—
that I'll be filled in about all the things I missed,

and that if, between this time and that one,
there is anyone who I learn to love,
I'll be able to find him there, too.

No doubt he'll be looking for me, expecting me
by the fruit trays. When the lights dim
and barkeeps announce last call,
angels will walk around with shawls
and formal coats draped over one celestial arm,
Inuit furs, togas and muumuus over the other,
and thank each guest for coming, as we trudge back out
to our coffins, to buckle up snug before
the colossally violent contraction
that will be the end of the world.

I will take my friend's hand and make one last pass
at the *hors-d'oeuvres* table. If he's a gentleman,
he'll open my coffin and wait for me to get in
before walking around to his own.
I'd be happy then, I think, settling in, knowing
that everything finally turned out all right.

Childhood Incident

I don't know why, but once, when I was twelve, my father
kicked me in the stomach. But that's too dramatic a way to say it.
I was sideways on the fifth stair and he was descending. I blocked
his path. He nudged his foot between my knees and stomach
and flipped me, rag doll, onto the foyer rug, a pile among sneakers,
mittens and discarded scarves. It didn't really hurt. But a friend
staying over saw the whole thing, and I recall the split instant
before anyone reacted: my friend's eyes on me, empty cisterns
unsure for the moment with what to fill. I guess I didn't know
how to react either. My friend and I held eyes a moment, passing
(if this doesn't sound too grand) between us a series of questions.
His eyes asked things mine couldn't answer; my eyes asked things
his couldn't, but for the merest instant—oh maybe we did it
in primary colors—we evaluated the scene like philosopher kings.
Here whole paradigms butted against each other. He wanted me
to explain. What could I explain? I wanted him to explain:
What happened to me? How did I get here? Do I hurt?
But there was no time for that. Suddenly an uproar engulfed us:
my mother, my friend, my father, me, too, I guess, everybody
wailing—recriminations, defenses, spasms of helplessness.

My father didn't cry, but every one else did. I cried. My mother
cried a lot. My friend cried though I don't know why. He cried
and pled with lawyerly conviction for my innocence. My father
left the house, and my mother sat with us in the den for hours
trying to explain in the gentlest and most loving possible terms
that my father was a nut. Then we all drank cocoa and went to bed.

That's the story. I know that's the story, I think. I'm sure that
once, when I was twelve, a friend, a little older, saw my father
kick me in the stomach from the stair where I was sitting, looking
down at him. My friend was in love with me. I know because
he told me every time we slept together. On weekends, when
my parents let him stay over. He was tall, thirteen, Spanish,
and watched me tumble with pitch eyes. In my bedroom afterward,
he wanted to hold me and tell me how mean my father was.
Can there be something beautiful about a twelve- and thirteen-
year-old sleeping together? My mother sat on the den chair, us
beneath her listening to her soothing words. It was as if we were
both her children, and given a stage to be wise, she told us a story
pitting love against carelessness. Then my friend and I
went upstairs and got each other off. She slept and my father
did whatever he had to do. That's the story. We clutched
each other's hairless bodies and whispered about the problem
of evil in the world. Then my friend went off to Christian Academy
and I never saw him again. I don't know what became of him, but
I do know that once, when he was thirteen, he saw the first guy
he ever slept with get kicked in the stomach by his father.

I also know that once when my father was forty-three he rushed
down the stairs, tying his tie at the time, came down the stairs
so quickly that he knocked me off the step. I know he saw me
lose my balance and fall down the steps. Or maybe he saw me
choose to lose my balance and let myself fall. It didn't
really hurt. Once when I was twelve I was sitting on a stair

and then I wasn't. And then there was a brief interval when
we each had to decide our version of what had happened.
Does it matter whether or not my father wore shoes at the time?
He wore black leather wing tips. My friend wanted
to hold me afterwards and tell me how mean my father was.
My father didn't stop dressing as we fought. Is that right?
My friend looked at me, and in that moment, his eyes told me
what had just happened: you're on the floor; you were kicked;
you hurt. Are the stairs a bad place to sit? Things were rough
with my parents. I know that as we sat with my mother
and she told us about my father and his intentions, she spoke
from a heap of broken dishes. I know that my parents
didn't know I was sleeping with my friend. Did they know?
If so, why did they let him stay over? Did they both know?
I certainly know that in the morning, there were four dollar bills
left for me, with a note scratched in red pen: "I'm sorry, love dad."
How did they get there? Did I feel better? That ended it.
That's the whole story. I know that's the story, I think. But
maybe it's not. What happened to me? How did I get here?
Do I hurt? Then we all drank cocoa and went to bed.

Blue-Black

standard poodle. His dog
had a seizure before

I was in the apartment two minutes:
pointed its snout to the ceiling

and froze up, stiffened, emitted
no high, penetrating whine. Just

silence. Later, in bed,
he explained it had been

beaten severely as a pup. But
that it was still a good dog. Nice

to be able to share the intimate details
of his dog's childhood

afterward, our pillow talk. He was
the first man I've ever been with who

faked an orgasm. Or maybe others
faked it better. Not to be

a cad, I asked. He kept his body
to the side and quietly explained that

"there wasn't a lot." "What's with
your dog," I said,

swinging my feet off the bed
to the pile of clothes on the floor, his

and mine. Poodle rescue. He'd hoped
to show the dog, even had

its hair cut right, undignified
for such a serious-looking animal.

You know, once you've had sex
with enough men, you learn to draw

reasonably accurate conclusions; this guy
was molested young. How

do I know that? I laced my boots
while he told me about the time he tried

to show the dog. It was too timid.
Wouldn't even enter the room; all

its training went out the window. Partially
I know by the behavior

he coaxed me into: the scripted
entrances and exits, the cues, props

to appear in one act, to be fitfully
discharged in another. His script:

neither violent nor elegant, but
his pleasure had no part in it. The dog

approached again
after I dressed, laid its black head

on my knee and looked up
with vulnerable eyes.

I cupped its head briefly in my lap
and stroked its ears.

He was out of the room by then
so I spoke to the animal. "You're

a good boy," I said. "A good boy."

How to Care for an Air Fern

The guy in floral was clear. I wasn't
listening. Instead, I was gazing

at this tiny tussle of green, almost
a fistful of sage. Growing! Alive—

despite the absence of roots. Floating
merely in a clay pot, a tuft of itself

peeking over the rim, as if to suggest
what's below was roots. You pull it out

and the mass is whole, tangled, undifferentiated
as a hairball, defying you to tell sun-side

from any other. *No roots?* No, the guy says,
no roots. *But how do I water it?*

I do not water it. I show it, though,
to anyone who comes by for any reason.

Thursday that's Dave, to return
my things after our break up. We do not

sleep together. I explain:
it's a seaweed. I think it grows.

We're silent a moment, wondering
where it finds substance to make

more of itself. I describe the opening scene
of *King Lear,* with an air fern:

the dotty old King and his daughter
pause with concern: *nothing*

will come from nothing. Dave
slings his gym bag over his shoulder

with surprisingly abrupt finality. He
has washed and folded my underwear.

Then his car backs out of the drive.
Do I feed it? I'm thinking about

a mister, Miracle-Gro solution. The guy
lifts the fern off the clearance table

where it's the only thing even remotely
like itself. No, no Miracle-Gro, he says.

No mister. Air currents. In Ohio
humidity's enough. *Enough?* Enough.

Okay. Saturday I show it to Steve. Steve
likes me so he pretends to be interested

longer than most people. *Yes,* I say,
I'd heard about them, read about them, but. . . .

I remove the fern from its pot, bounce it up
on my palm, then return it to the pot

upside down. Steve takes it out, feels it, then
puts my hand in his. He wants us to go away

for a weekend. *Who would look after
the air fern?* Apparently

it's not a concern. He hugs me extra long
before he leaves, to make sure

I know he likes me. *What about
sunlight?* Don't worry. Put it in a window;

it will be fine. *Should I turn it, rotate it,
exhale on it every few days? I guess*

grow sticks are out of the question? No,
he says. Look, he says, no grow sticks. No

water. It's only two dollars. You just
leave it. You don't need to do

anything. Just leave it alone and enjoy it.
He shoves it at me. I look down

at the little fern, waiting in its clay pot.
There's no going back now; I've as good

as bought it. But for a moment
I feel an inkling of pity: the directions,

simple, explicit, and yet the one thing
I'll be completely unable to do.

Time and Place

Because I seem unable to get a handle
on either, I have been tempted lately to confuse
time and place. It starts like this: you call

wanting to come by tomorrow. Six o'clock
would be an empty parking lot in Flagstaff,
sundown everywhere, sky busted up, busted open

belly, red and white for miles. Nine would be
Holmdel Park in May: in my hometown,
you wouldn't have heard of it. Except

we'd be there, on the hill above the lake,
bower hidden by the land's rise and fall.
The problem, of course, is that these places

recall other times, and the present becomes
impossibly layered. Somewhere between six
and Holmdel comes (becomes) the fear

that I can't love you and that, all these years later
(measured as you'd expect in an accumulation
of place), I no longer have the fortitude

to leave anyone. What happens then?
On the phone, we agree seven thirty. You will
"spend the night," which is a time

that involves a place, and a history: wakeful nights
next to men with whom there is
something unsaid. All those unspent nights.

Do you want to share a time and place
if it requires sharing a history? Recollections
of snoring bodies like a personal affront,

backs big and distant as drive-in movie screens,
and me tensed, blinking, wondering
what in that place could pass the time.

Do I want you to come over? Of course. But
perhaps in another place and time. I might say
I'm not in the right place for this, for us; and,

it's not you, just that the timing isn't right.
Except both would be lies, or at the very least,
conveniences. Imagine, in a black vacuum, no up,

no down, not even on the same plane: two men
(helmets, space suits) holding opposite ends
of a phone line. "Can I come over?" crackles

through static, in a context beyond "where" (no
common referent), outside "when" (some blather
about Einstein, and both of us implicated

in the speed of light). Then, lover, you'd hear
my answer clear through the ether: "Of course,"
then, "no," and "I want you; I want you; I want you."

Bioluminescence

To attract prey. Or indicate fear, pain. It might
well radiate from the chest, from within the bell
of the ribs, slight at first, and warming to flesh
and pink until, at full bore, each gives off
his own light, letting everyone see into the body—
a single dark mass within the glow
for the heart, tapering to gray where arteries thin.

Summer nights around cities, humans pulse on—
slowly—and off, appearing and disappearing
on sidewalks, illuminating around them
their companions, drawing briefly moths, flies,
the bugs reflecting the light, small meteors
brushing past the sun. Couples might glimmer
in sympathy, might warm together

toward passion or wrath, or criticize each other
for failing to get the timing right.
Perhaps if some left turn in our history
had demanded another mode of communication,
we might glow when we cluster, to express safety,
draw others: families on porches
kindling each other to brightness, except
for an outcast teen who lingers alone
near the car, marked only by the red dot
of her cigarette.

Or perhaps it would be something to control,
a physical process seldom acknowledged,
and a school-age child might be sent
to the nurse for it, not to be scolded, exactly,
like the precocious girl in everyone's middle school
who left class because she got her period,
which, though secretly curious, we all laughed at.
And how awful to have it pointed out that first time,
before you noticed it yourself, that you were glowing. . . .

No doubt there would be hierarchies—
brightness, color, how long
you could hold your glow. It would play
some unlikely role in mating.

And perhaps, like our voices or the way
we touch, it would be something else singular
about us to be remembered as we fade, that those
who love us most could differentiate in any dark.

Holding Hands

I was eighteen watching a movie with other students in a dorm
the first time a man held my hand. His name was Shawn.
He wore large yellow Mickey Mouse slippers and perfectly round
wire rims; his hair was jet black with a bleached forelock.

Someone shut the lights; someone else flipped on the VCR;
a pipe and lighter were passed around. And then Shawn, who had

flopped on the floor beside me, reached over and intertwined
my fingers in his. The movie, Disney, I think, seemed long—
very long, incredibly long, even—because of course as soon as
Shawn touched me I became instantly, completely, manifestly

excited. Thankfully the room was dark. I didn't know Shawn.
Not well. And I wasn't attracted to him. But no man had ever

touched me like that before. I gave no sign of pleasure. In fact,
neither Shawn nor I acknowledged that we were holding hands—
not through the entire film, no turn, no shy smile, no movement
of any sort. We both studiously stared at the television screen

as if we were going to be tested on it afterwards. Still I was fixated:
each of his fingers felt particular, erotic, slightly lubricated

by sweat, like an independent sensory organ. Each felt hot
and disturbingly organic. And the whole time others were around,

passing the pipe, making cracks at the screen. None of them
seemed to be aware. Was this a scandal of human sexuality,

this semi-public arousal? Was it better because they were there?
Months passed before Shawn and I felt brave enough to kiss,

and even then, some time longer before we'd wake up sprawled
across each other, before we wasted entire college days
stuck to his dorm-room bed as to flypaper, and months after that
before it ended—as it had to, strange German-arthouse-looking

boy to whom I was never attracted—but none of it, none of it
lasted as long as that movie, the name of which I can't remember,

the endless hours I sat as still as possible in the dark, thankful
under a long t-shirt. There was love after, with other men,
and sex after, with him, but it never seemed to last those eternities,
and it never—is this possible?—seemed to feel so good.

Like the Back of My Hand

It was only that I noticed the joints—the larger ones—
on my fingers, that they resemble knots in an old oak,
and below them each hair a pinprick, the skin riddled
like an old dart board, and thought, incomprehensibly,
this is the same hand I had with me thirty-odd years ago,
like a pair of scissors or salad tongs that hasn't worn out
or snapped or gotten lost, and is still pretty good.
And my knuckles, pale mountains, the cracked tops
dusted with snow—dryness, I guess—bled white

when the bones press against the skin, realized
how beaten up they are, though not those of a fighter,
never in fact impacted with a jaw, a wall, or clutched
a roll of quarters for ballast, never scraped into the guts
of a machine to make it work. But still, how scarred,
fractured, the kind of terrain Eliot treks through
at the end of *The Waste Land*. And thought,
what a strange weathered thing is attached to me,
strange leathern thing that might fit by a gutter

in November, unremarkable among gray, brown
and orange leaves: crumpled like them, small claw
curling inward, withered chicken foot. But here,
still here, after thirty-odd years, and still undeniably
functional, practical, and near, near though strange.
But not strange as I lift it, not strange as I
bring it upward, where it can do what nothing else,

what no one else seems able to do—how gently,
how reassuringly it knows to touch my face.

Adwaitya and the Fruit Fly

If this were a joke, the punch line—
"out wait ya"—would be said

by the fruit fly. If it were a myth, a god
would be brought in to explain

why humans have only seventy years. If
a parable, Adwaitya and the fly

would come across a fallen apple
and argue whether it was dinner

or a world. If a fable, they'd meet
at dawn when the fly was young,

and Adwaitya, ancient in his middle age,
would whet it to the discoveries

of day. When they met again at dusk,
Adwaitya would listen silent

to the wisdom of his elder. If found
in Ovid, a shepherd

would be made to live an hour as each
to learn that experientially

there's no such thing as an hour.
If a novel, the fruit fly would be passionate,

dissolute, would pitch his fiery chariot
too close to the Earth. Adwaitya below

would ponder the anchored ground
with each hesitant step. And if it were

a poem, Adwaitya would symbolize
the requirements of living, slow

breathing as the world undergoes
irreversible change. If a poem,

Adwaitya would be commuting,
working, and all necessity

that crowds the heart. And the fruit fly—
a figure for the poet—would buzz

at his tasks, trying madly
to hone himself to carefulness. And

the great tortoise would block
his efforts. And the fruit fly

would buzz in his mounting hysteria.
The tortoise would take a full two hours

to ask, "And just how do you suppose
you're going to get by me?"

Ambition

I want to write a body. I'd like to discover
some combination of words which can incarnate
a man in his seat, as if during a reading
I addressed the poem to a room full save
for a single empty chair. Let's say I was riveting.
The audience looked their myriad ways:
some at me, forgetting they were looking at me;
some down at their toes, their knees;
all having relinquished sight in a way the sighted
almost never do. And in their midst, in a chair
between two of them, a miracle happens.

With the first words, the auditorium dust
begins to coalesce, to take shape into toes,
each topped with a few black hairs.
I finish a line, and feet are there—
hairy ankles ending like candles, in a flame
burning upward. The poem is in paragraph stanzas.
By the time I finish two—sweeping the audience
with my eyes, meeting all the faces I can—
a simple metal foldout chair, center, three rows back,
holds a pair of knees, the flesh and fibers
thickening to thighs as I pause
before the third stanza.

Okay, then someone in the audience coughs.
For a moment, all our attentions

are shifted, and I waver around his midsection;
what was beginning to twitch with life—
an itch on his calf though there aren't yet
hands to scratch it—begins to loosen,
as if the particulate matter might wash
back into the room, break up or burn off like fog.

But I push on. My voice is firm; I retake
the audience, and again, his legs
solidify. I'm on the fourth stanza now,
and there he is, belly button down.
Of course I am writing him naked, so
it's a good thing all eyes are looking off
or the women and children in the audience
might get upset. But they are upset anyway
because many of the poems I have read this evening
use transparent bug metaphors to talk about gay sex.
This poem doesn't upset them, though; this one
has their eyes bruised, their mouths wet;
this one has them seated way back in the last row
of the movie theaters of their minds, sunk deep
into plush seats, barely conscious as they watch
in the dark. They don't notice the genitals
lying on the only empty seat, or how
the muscled stomach reaches upward,
curves in and out for abdominals, slopes out slightly

for pectorals—how each syllable from my mouth
seems to leap, to become a seed sprouting
out of his chest a curly black hair.
They don't notice, and I don't tell them. I read on.

I begin the last stanzas to a silent room.
Now my mouth is wet, too. Here is where I do it,
here is where I introduce the killer image that recalls
and rounds up earlier strands in the poem. I say color;
they see color. I control when all of us breathe.
I speak, and one of the arms at his sides reaches down
to scratch his calf, and a face begins to take shape
from the mass of filaments reaching up
from his neck: hard jaw line, black stubble,
nose, cheekbones, the smile of a man who knows
that he is the only person in the room naked
and doesn't care. His eyes remain closed.
Opening them will take the final line. But
he's already palpably there. I can practically
smell his skin from the podium. So I pause—
at the dash before the final lines, my last wind up,
and throw the best pitch I've got.

Those who have been looking at their knees
now look up, and those who have been looking forward
tilt their heads back. In that instant

he opens his black eyes right at me. I notice
his lips, the openness of his body.
I am emptied and crushed by desire.

Then the audience exhales. And with a sad but gentle,
even generous smile, he nods goodbye
before vanishing, turning to water vapor
and lifting into the air above us.
Now I exhale, too. Maybe next time, I think;
he was cute, and I'm pretty sure he liked me.
But the audience doesn't care. Someone lifts her purse
off the empty seat. People applaud like they do
at the end of a poetry reading. Then they stand,
and we all go home. Some of us go alone.

Two Apples

1.
I remember eating an apple when I was young
like most people remember their first kiss.
Red Delicious. Wine red. Red
                              and cut
before my eyes into slices, splayed like a flower,
as if the apple itself—the thickened petals
of a certain rose—
                    opened on the plate
to a flesh bloom. I remember the taste
of the first slice in my mouth, the living
cinnamon, my small hand lifting
                                the crescent
to my lips, and then lifting another crescent,
then another. Upstairs, by the banister, the rails
before my face like prison bars,
                            I ate
not one apple but two. Or three. More. Not
a flower but a mound, the pile of petals at the foot
of a fallen rose: not a five-petalled
                          apple flower
but the roses we have bred to be monstrous
with petals, a child born with eight or ten
fingers on each hand, waving them
                              nervously
in the crib. I ate till I was sick and the three

[67]

brothers behind me burst into laughter. Then
they began to fall out over who'd clean it up.

2.
I went fifteen years without eating an apple.
Who else can say that but Eve?
Fifteen years without the hard crunch that now
I prefer above all things, the hardest of apples,
the lifted flesh that leaves a wound
glazed with juice. Even thinking about it now

I feel longing—a chilled Granny Smith,
the tartness to the highest pitch of pleasure
before pleasure turns: the belted note
that would be a scream in any context
other than song. It's been too long
now, when it's been about three days.

And yet once it was fifteen years.
I think of Eve among the crabs and wild
species, after she'd been kicked out—
after we had been. How all fruits
must have been a pleasure to her, a privilege
back then before pesticides, before

supermarkets. Unthinkable: to have to wait
for the fall to enjoy apples. But even then,

in the world's first falls, in the autumnal wealth
of squashes, now big with Abel and holding
the hand of jittery Cain, she must have
looked suspiciously at apple trees, their fruits

clustered with a mysterious tightness
to the branch. Knowledge merely of
how this or that apple tasted, she must have
told herself, ignoring the mother's intuition,
that if her womb could deliver a body of good,
she already held the hand of evil.

So maybe she went fifteen years like me,
interim informed by both good and evil,
before she stretched her middle-aged bones
to a laden limb, a bough bright with half-dozen
apples, and plucked one, and ate.
Would the voice of God boom again

from the heavens, the earth groan deep
in its cavernous womb? Or maybe hers
was another fear: that this was somehow
that other tree, that she'd stumbled unawares
back to the Garden, and so now, after so much
life, would be constrained to live

                              even longer.

3.
A man was involved. Tall, thin, English,
late twenties, long black hair in a pony tail.

He gave me the fruit; I was hungry, so I ate.
I had just met him on Vorhees Lawn

under a row of hundred-year-old oaks,
the manicured lawn with three rows

of oaks, columns in a Greek temple
with a canopy of springtime green.

I was just taking a walk. Tiana dazzled
among the oaks: she, tall, Nordic, cheek bones

like shields on either side of her face, she
was the Goddess Nike, white victory,

nineteen with round hips and azure eyes.
Tiana saw him and whispered, "I think

he's cute; do you think he's cute," then
walked up to where he sat against a tree

reading a small book, a moment later
motioning me over with her hand.

I didn't go until she called me, and then
there was no polite way to refuse.

Tiana flirted so easily that soon they were
both flirting, and I was, too. *Just*

laughing with them. I am not a flirt.
He invited us back to his dorm room,

the three of us on the edge of his bed
for hours: I sat quiet, listening to their chatter

until it was evening, until it was nearly
midnight. Then he asked with his graduate-

student boldness if I wanted to spend the night.
He looked directly at me, full eye contact

and a half grin. *I don't recall ever saying yes.*
Tiana shrugged and lifted herself off the bed.

She collected her things while I was stuttering
to reply. And soon she was gone, passing

soundlessly out of the room, white Goddess
drifting away from mortals, leaving

in silence the three of us: him, me,
and the bright Granny Smith on his desk.

I did see it there, but I would not
have asked for it. It was then that he offered,

picked it up and held it out to me.
And how could I refuse it from his hand?

The next morning, I recall walking home
through the oaks of Vorhees, light filtering

through the canopy, a tiny human dwarfed
in a Temple of Gods. *I still didn't know*

what I had done, or why I had done it,
or why it was that I hadn't done it before.

The Colossus at Rhodes

for a wedding

1.

In a profound rumbling, he tumbles—the earth-
quake and storm resonating just the right frequency
for brass to twist and sway, as if for a moment he were
dancing, or wobbling uneasily trying to regain his footing.
But instead of falling over—his feet, his ankles
never leave the harbor rock—he falls apart.
First an arm seems to shudder, to wrench itself
forward, then a crack at the elbow announces the first
dissolution, and the forearm falls to the shore.
Now cracks begin to appear everywhere;
and light—the streaks of lightning ripping across
the harbor sky—reflects bluish white inside them.
But still he does not fall, still he suspends shivering
in a dance, an ecstasy of movement, his inside
manifestly lit and pulsing with fire, Colossus
with innards of light, no longer able to contain
his own brightness.
                    And we are there—
we are at the harbor, where it bows deep into Rhodes.
We are old and can remember (was it eighty years ago?)
the celebration, the drums and the regatta sailing
between his ankles, speeches to Helios, invocations
to the sun. As we watch now this flickering,
the elongated instant, we do not believe

he will ever come down—despite the second arm now
cracking at the shoulder, the hand swinging out
to the ocean, falling soundlessly into the black water.
This event—we know even as we see it, even
before he comes down—this marks the end
of our lives, our era. The Colossus seems to nod
in agreement, his head dipping slightly forward,
and then, with a tear that pierces the thunder,
the head tumbles down from his body, into the bay.

2.
Morning five hundred years later: the sun
over the harbor mouth brightens the ruins.
The head under the harbor for generations, but
feet and ankles still poke up from either shore
like book ends, and on the beach lie fragments
of the shoulder; the crook of a knee cap;
an upturned hand in which two teenagers sit.
They hold hands there, in the open palm of the God.
He is broken like any man, but they are young
and do not bother to differentiate love from desire,
and find in his brokenness a comfortable place
to whisper and examine sea shells. Her knee
brushes his when she swings her legs, over the ridge
of the pinky finger. They who now kiss
in the ruin, who discover a little love in this disaster
of fragmentation, how shocking to discover

that they are also us.
                    We have spent the day
playing with the pieces, chasing each other
in the harbor sand. You hid behind a length
of thigh and struck the hollow brass so it thudded
low and resonant when I came near to you.
Hasn't this wreckage always been here?
Didn't your mother sit pregnant on top of his foot,
gazing into the future? As a boy, my grandfather
used to climb the ankles, like everyone's grandfather;
he stood atop twisted metal, king of the mountain.
We have built our home in this wreckage;
we have made love there. Funny to think it ever had
another shape, that it was meant to resemble a man—
or more than that, a man who could contain
lightning within his form, Helios, God
of the sun, imminent over the harbor mouth.

3.
Legend has it that in 653 AD, the first Caliph
of the Umayyad dynasty carried away the pieces
and sold them. But who cares about that now
when through the murky lens of the water
the upturned head has seen the introduction
of satellites, blinking red lights among the stars?
A man walks the shore, a vacation spot
with small bungalows nestled in the trees.

The man has plans, blueprints; these are neither
on drafting paper nor drive; they are part of a memory
so old there's no way he can be remembering it—
an image of wholeness that corresponds to little
he knows or has seen in the world. Yet the memory
is there, part of his vocabulary, like a word
whose derivation has been lost for centuries.
And it is nothing less than a miracle
that he is not alone.
                              That man is also us,
and his companion comes armed with the same vision.
How delightful that we meet each other here, too—
with mallets and rivets in hand. See how
they compare notes, set together to forge
new legs, to use hydraulic lifts, perhaps, that will
raise the head from the water. We squint and see
a brass figure rising behind metal scaffolding.
The Colossus was something, but even if they
can't quite bring it back, isn't the attempt itself
no less a wonder of the world? See how they
kneel together on the sand, plot a form
to embody, to contain the sun; how they
know it, formulating it without language;
how their eyes, our eyes, are gentle with power.
It's no small thing they make, no small thing they build.

In Memoriam: Ginger

Ginger, whom I did not like to look at, or talk to, to whom
I was polite only by an act of will, is dead, dead and gone.
Vacant now: her apartment, the only one in the basement—
by the laundry and the small storage cubbies that the landlord
throws in free. I saw the ambulance, noticed it a few weeks ago
when I shut my lights for sleep: blue and red flashing
through the blinds. I looked out to see Ginger's daughter—
apartment three, other side of the building—walk doggedly
back and forth on the lawn, from her apartment door back out
to the curb. I didn't know then it was for Ginger. Ask not.
That knowledge came later, when I told Aline—first floor,
decorates the hall for Christmas, Easter, the seasons generally,
plastic snowflakes, that sort of thing—that she looked nice.
Aline said it was for Ginger, the funeral held earlier that morning.

I wondered why I hadn't been invited, but then I remembered
that Aline is kind to everyone, and I, a snob, had rejected Ginger.

My difficulty with Ginger wasn't due to her weird body,
though that bothered me, her weird breasts hanging down nearly
to her waist. I'm not saying this was her fault. Or her laugh—
I want to write "cackle"—how loud it was, how I could see
when she laughed that her teeth were cracked, blackened,
that her middle-aged gums had burned-out spaces.
The landlord once tried to evict Ginger for having a cat.
The whole building was up in arms because others had cats, too.
I'm the only tenant with a dog; I didn't get involved.

Even though the entire basement—laundry area, cubbies—
smelled like her catbox, the landlord eventually relented.
But none of this especially disturbed me about Ginger.
Certainly not enough to hope she'd be forced to leave.

No, the problem was her speech. The way she spoke
sent my shoulders up, made me back away nearly instinctively,
as from an object that cast my own humanity into doubt. Ginger
slurred her words incredibly, tortured and twisted each word
out of her mouth, each syllable like Blake's tyger, violently
hammered in the furnace of her gullet. At first I thought
it was an Ohio drawl, but the more I heard it—scraping
chalkboards sonorous by comparison—the more I realized
it was all Ginger and no Ohio. I'd never heard anyone
do that to language before: no alcohol, no organic instigation
that I could see, just Ginger opening her mouth hugely,
gaping her mouth like a cavern at dusk delivering a nearly
unending stream of bats—the deep, cavernous mouth
guarded by only a few shards of teeth. It was horrible.
I kept my eyes down on the washer when she spoke,
my hands on the machine as if feeling for psychic contact
with the laundry. I didn't understand a word she said.

I thought to ask Pat—second floor, across the hall from me,
clutters the area outside her door with boxes of scarves—
how Ginger died. Pat wouldn't judge me for asking,
even though it's not my business. Or is it? These people

with whom I live, whose sounds I know nearly as well
as my own—whose business if not mine? The woman
whose living room abuts my bedroom: I know what she sings
to help her baby sleep. She knows the universe
of pet names I have for my dog. What could be more
embarrassing than that? No more awkwardly intimate
or unchosen than those people into whom I was born,
though here with the surprising element of tolerance—

except for Ginger, who I did not tolerate, unless avoidance
too is a brand of tolerance, maybe tolerance's last resort.

Ginger's door has been left open; she died midmonth,
so her clothes, her things have the space a few more weeks.
After that someone new will come, and with or without effort,
that person will know and become known—will enlarge
this thing that isn't a family, that is both more and less
than friendship, our daily unacknowledged intimacy. How odd
that it could be anyone. But that's for later. Now, the apartment
is still Ginger's, the empty space a collective—if temporary—
testament to her memory. I can see quite clearly inside,
her things half packed in boxes for Goodwill, the undusted
closed blinds. Almost nothing, finally, of whatever it is
that Ginger was: mother and tenant, I guess; maker,
if nothing else, of a sound that has vanished from the world.

Purgatory

In this version of the afterlife I am forced
to reenact every failed moment of my
earthly existence until I get each one right
as adjudicated by a panel of cranky angels.
They are not interested in my successful moments
which they largely take credit for.

The failures began when I was small, even perinatal.
I opened my mouth too soon, nearly
drowning in amniotic fluid. The video pauses,
and the angels shake their heads, knit
their fingers on the long white table
in front of them. Wings sag.
Then two burly Italians come over
and shoulder me toward a dressing room
in which I am forced to put on a wet suit.
The next hour is awful, as I must press my lips shut
despite jerking motion and the fascinating things
I notice about my mother's birth canal.
The studio audience laughs at my first few attempts,
played for them on a large screen—
the gurgle and sputter as amniotic fluid
courses repeatedly into my gullet. But they applaud warmly
when I finally make it through. On the wall above the angels
there's a big picture of me naked, with a halo and wings.
The angels nod approvingly, a bell sounds, and the toes
on the picture light up.

Then come other challenges:
the pet turtle I killed by leaving it trapped
in a milk crate in the July sun (baked him
in his shell, my brother said); and a year later,
digging up said turtle in his Danish Butter Cookie tin.
The spirit of the turtle watches dourly from the front row.
The fire I caused in the backyard by lighting up
a failing report on Prince Henry the Navigator—
surprising because I didn't think anyone
knew about that, also because the angels
seem indifferent to my failure to use more than one source.
Some of my earthly errors continue to trip me up
even after hours of attempts,
so I am allowed to call on other dead for help.
Dickens reminds me to spend money on friends
and to avoid work in counting houses. Lawrence
coaches me on how to talk to my mother.
Whitman seemed good to help with those moments
I was unable to repress distaste for humanity
but finally proves a little standoffish in his own right.

After what feels like an eternity,
the halo on the wall lights up, too,
and the audience cheers as a pair of wings descends
to the stage. The angels majestically float over
and take up positions, a few on each side of me.
The audience goes wild now; hosannas are sung.

I get really excited, too, because
somewhere off I hear a car ignition
and a drum roll begins to play.
Then the angels raise their heavenly arms, balloons
drop, and a brand new Toyota Camry, champagne
on tan, keyless entry, slowly rolls onto the stage.
And the best part, lover, is that you're there, too,
behind the wheel, still somehow with me
after decades and decades. A near miracle after the catalogue
of missteps and miscalculations,
the one thing I assuredly got right.

Adam's Punishment

Through the kitchen window, over a sink
full of yesterday's dishes: imagine—

morning, and you stand there, your robe
slung lazily around you—

imagine the saplings on the first day
after their planting: framed by that window,

newly wet in the April sunrise, fifty
of them shoulder to shoulder, straight

as any Roman line. Their branches are
bare, black, spindly, like letters typeset

into the new day. Sticking up
in five rows on the side field, they spell

possibility, over and over that
same word. You start the water now

and squeeze dish soap into the stream.
Turn your attention back

to the morning's task: bubbles rise, cover
the dishes, hot water rising under them.

But no, you lift your head again—
they are framed by everything, as if

your life were mere context for a still life:
Orchard through Kitchen Window.

The back of your head, dishes, counter-
top and cabinets, all are silhouetted;

all contour's lost in favor of what shines
through the glass, owns every trace

of its first exposure to sun—
each tree an antenna picking up

a signal from the sky, finding music
pent in the clouds, which will now

rumble its bass under this earth.
But there's no time for that this morning.

You are not a silhouette.
Your hand begins in clockwise motion

around the rim of a dinner plate.
The only music comes from the radio, half

static from another room. So you move on
with the dishes, stack plates, bowls.

You dip the scrub pad back into the water.
But it's no use, is it? The sun is up,

fully up, and you can't avoid the arc
of branches, how they reach skyward—

so the trees become rows of children
forking their arms in a stretch, a teacher

somewhere off guiding motions after a nap.
All the knowledge, you think, all the good

and evil in the world yet to unfold, unfurl
in their heads. All those hands, you think,

how their work will blossom into clusters—
how their work will eventually be ready

for the hands of the world. Or the trees
are magicians, you think, that might

pull anything from their sleeves—
handkerchiefs, rabbits, flowers, doves

rising up, filling the air above the bare
branches. Or apples. They're magicians

who can find twenty-five years of bright
apples hidden in the white ruffles

at their forearms, with peat, water, and sun,
apples enough to blanket this acre of earth.

In a moment you will reach in your hand
and lift the stop, hear dirty water drain.

It will be time to move on because
you are no silhouette, because life

requires you to work so that you can eat.
But for now you look out the window,

and imagine the trees, and imagine
the pleasure of planting them

yourself. What could the Old
Testament, or any testament, have

to compare to that? Thank God,
you think. Thank God we are mortal.

Stark Brothers

I pass by the catalogue all day: sixteen
glossy pages of perfect fruit. Not
as in a still life: no bowl, no knife, but
branch, cluster, fruit held as tightly as fists
and dripping, glistening as if to suggest
fresh rain, more than morning dew. The colors
are perfectly as they ought to be, in variegated
imperfection: the mottling white rings
on the tart green of a Granny Smith, the peaches
demonstrating how orange at dusk
fades to brown, and the light hairs, too,
nearly palpable to a hand run over the page.

It's all there. The grapes that Faustus
sent for from across continents; plums
as dark and sweet as sin in the underworld;
enough perfect apples to fill a whole town
with knowledge of good and evil, and immortality,
and an artist's sense of the color spectrum.
The catalogue, on the table by my door,
is a kind of bible of the moment;
as I come and go I give the book its due.

For all this temptation, there is a price
list, and there are charts. These—the black-
and-white insert—beckon, too, because
the planning's so easy. Charts to choose

spacing, root stock, high or low vigor
varieties, any diploid in its season. And given
the cost of all we want, jewelry, or cars,
or homes, or prestige, or those things
other people have, it is an inhabitable
irony that the symbol of desire itself
should be so cheap: ten dollars a tree.

Listen: the work of our hands may be
a conscious choice—as measured as a grid
of trees—or it may correspond to everything
else about us in ways we ourselves
are least likely to understand. Our ideas
may lead one to another, as a seedling
grows close to the tree, or they may be
unfolding manifestations of an initial impulse.
There may be maps for the grandest accidents—
for the broadleaf forests that used to cover
the eastern United States, covered the body
of the continent like hair. There may be maps

of ourselves, rolled scrolls that elucidate
the pathways through the self, as an eagle
over a northern wood might view highways—
maps that to see would be a better
afterlife than any I've heard proposed,
the only thing that could release us

willingly from our bodies, our lives. Otherwise
we might linger stubborn, arms crossed
in the corpse, pigheaded at the foot of God.

       Catalogue, phone call, Master Card: the first steps
       through any wood are deceptively easy,
       as the light takes a while to change, as wind
       off the open world still moves us forward.
       Perhaps we are always poised before our choices
       and it's only in continuing to make them
       that we have made them at all. I linger
       at my catalogue: thinking about the perfection
       of its pictures, imagining the cool
       snap off the branch, pressure on the lips,
       the crunch of the very first bite.

The Trees Arrive

Dirtless, leafless, nearly limbless in clear plastic,
they are the merest of selves: shy
girls who have not yet tried the shine
of their smile; boys who look down

when you try to discover the color
of their eyes. They are rolled together
like an auditorium of such children
standing to say the pledge. But it will happen.

Green spears burst into purples
wildly larger than the seed's space
to dream them. A firework's a tight
honeycomb of powder and power—

a softball that could crack the garage window,
its secrets instantly ended by a razorblade's
attempt to relieve the pressure
of its mechanism. In other words

the future's inside, a mystery
of the self and how it's grafted to form
a characteristic thing. The children
go their ways into the world. The bright flash

of a solid break and balls scatter
on the felt. Years later, one of the kids

leans in a pool hall, cigarette dangling off his lip;
he remembers no other self. The subtle knot

that makes us what? Is that what's in these boxes:
flesh notched into, grafted onto soul?
Certainly an orchard's in the box, a colossal
pop-up book. An innocent flip and the spine

spreads so wide the reader finds himself
lost in the trees that rise up around him.
Yesterday he sat with classmates in an auditorium.
Tomorrow in a pool hall, he'll watch smoke

curl in the half light over a table. An orchard's
in the box; a world's in the auditorium. Fire's
in the firework: inside the package
with the black cat, a neighborhood blazing

on a clear night. A child kneels to unwrap it
in a secret corner of the garage. Smells
of oily rag and petrol hunch and leer
from shadows all around him. Pandora's

there, too, glancing sideways
with shared apprehension. School bell—
kids scatter out two sets of auditorium doors
as if struck by a cue ball. At the end of the day,

each will find hope remaining in a coat pocket,
except for those who won't. I'm there, too,
shyly pulling copper staples one by one
to crack the back panel—

a gate thrown wide, and a dust storm
of mustangs rushes through, flinging it
right off its hinges. The cowboy retreats, nearly
falls backward. Only his right hand

keeps the hat on his head. Pandora's hair's
blown wide as a spider web by the purple
scrolls of mischief blooming all around her,
a rush of flowers, pyrotechnic lilacs

sprung up in long clusters. Hear the break crack.
But no: this box is quiet. The hanging panel reveals
roots as tentative, as ostensibly taken with authority
as children with their hands over their hearts.

Okay. I stand, and cover mine, too:
I'll pledge to this—it's all the flag I need. A stack
of bills sits unpaid on the counter. They won't, can't
stay there long. The unlit firework beckons.

Every mustang's potential miles. It's life, isn't it?
Sometimes patient in its latency, sometimes

so detailed and loud as it bursts over the house
that the dog hurls herself like a battering ram

against the back porch screen, again and again
throws her shoulder. Soon she'll burst into the night—
the sky's purple and fading; the fields spread out
north, east, and west. She'll run and keep on running.

Not Children

I know. But let me describe how gently
I pulled apart the plastic, the cowl, how the plastic
split at its stapled seam, revealing wet, olive-
colored bark. I'm not exaggerating when I say
I've never seen anything more beautiful
in the human body, though it did most resemble
human skin. Let me talk about the winnowing
of fingers through barrows of the local clay
cut with composted horse manure, fingers, arms
up to the elbow, sifting, mixing, breaking up
clumps of the compost, feathering it over
heavy clay, aerating, leavening, darkening.
Let me describe the speckled brown:
how the mixed medium had richness, felt good
on the palms, soft on the soft parts of the body.
Now imagine yourself bending with me,
lifting a tree from the plastic, extricating a single
sapling from the bundle, how your fingers
relearn gentleness unlacing the hair of the roots
from other roots, how in the manner of a mother
washing a child, you touch the most vulnerable
parts of the tree, the places where it would be
frighteningly easy to choke off life. And now
let's stand together, lift it from the plastic
and wash it down again, the pressure of the hose
blocked by your palm, so water falls easily
on the young trunk. Its place in the world is prepared;

bring it over, rest it in, as if into human arms.
The earth will love the thing no more than we do.
And now imagine yourself with me
stepping back from the planted sapling. Feel
how you steep and rise, how your chest fills
and then the slow, steady release of air.

Greening Song

There's a singer in the orchard—hidden among the new
leaves, the pale slender green of the shoots. I hear him

at all hours, along with other sounds of this country living:
the stray Harley chopping past and a four AM flight route

that shakes the new-growing corn. Yes, there's corn, too—
barely half a foot high—and when night's chilly,

morning leaves a single bead in the whirl of each plant.
Maybe the singer in the orchard croons also to the corn:

the trees around him fuller now, like trees, and beyond—
acres and acres of feed corn, with a clear glistening

in the vortex of each. Six weeks back, a neighbor
asked me what all the stakes were out there for.

"You building a barn or something?" It's no surprise
she didn't know—because nights were quiet then,

his voice nearly hushed as winter. He's louder now, as
each of the buds along branch and trunk become

fringed with fuzz and split red, as tiny red-tipped leaves
unfold. Or maybe it was the rows of soybeans

on the neighboring farm that started him, the simple shrug
of each seedling. Whatever the cause, he's louder now:

so loud Harleys don't quite drown him out anymore
and the drop of light inside each corn plant vibrates

with his tremolo in the early hours. With a big grin,
big Jim across the street asked when I was going to

give him apples. "You sure gonna have enough," he said.
Jim's heard it, too, Friday afternoons when he plays ball

with some buddies on his drive. A few days earlier,
I'd seen Jim and his friends pointing to the orchard:

they'd heard him, and he distracted from their play.
Well, they'd better get used to it because he's only

getting louder. By August next year, his voice may wave
through mature corn stalks like a storm wind. And that's

feed corn, which is stiff, strong. By August a few years
forward, planes may hear him as they descend

to the local airport. The orchard will be shaded by then,
the tree canopy blocking much of the sun, so the singer

will wander openly, throwing his hands over his head
like an opera star. It'll get so people will think

there's a show going on in there. They'll pull their SUVs
up to the edge of my lawn, get out, and look around.

"What's all this music?" they'll say. "At first, it was barely
a whisper," I'll say. "At first, it wasn't anything at all."

Notes

The cover image, Frederic Leighton's "The Garden of the Hesperides" (1892), depicts the daughters of Hesperus, God of Evening. In the classical story, Hera asks the Hesperides to guard the golden apples, a wedding present from the Goddess Earth. Leighton replaces the dragon of the original myth with a serpent.

Lines 47 and 48 of "Had I Been There, Had It Been Me" quote Kent's ardor in the first scene of *King Lear*.

"Pig Auction," which recalls the annual Greene County, Ohio Fair, is for Steve Green. Line 7 of this poem alludes to *Macbeth*, 5.5.23-25.

Lines 21 through 24 of "Beetle Orgy" describe the Raku-firing process. "Beetle Orgy" is for Paul Simmons.

In order to bear a child, a disguised Tamar later seduces the father of Er and Onan, Genesis 38:14-18.

Adwaitya, an Aldabran tortoise, was believed to have been 250 years old when he died on March 23, 2006.

"The Colossus at Rhodes" is for the marriage of Mathew Lewis and Kitty Potter, and the marriage of Daniel Webster and Gina Guiducci.

The image in section 2, lines 37 and 38 of "Two Apples" echoes *Paradise Lost*, 9:782-784.

Line 24 of "The Trees Arrive" alludes to Donne's "The Ecstacy."

Acknowledgments

Grateful acknowledgment is made to the journals in which these poems previously appeared:

Agni (online edition): "In Memoriam: Ginger" and "Like the Back of My Hand"

AkronArtMuseum.org: "Incantation"

Bellingham Review: "Asked What He's So Afraid of, He Pauses"

Blue Moon Review: "Blue-Black"

Cimarron Review: "Why God Hated Onan"

580 Split: "Greening Song" and "Ambition"

Malahat Review: "How to Care for an Air Fern" and "Pig Auction"

Mid-American Review: "Not Children"

Ninth Letter: "Purgatory"

North American Review: "Terro Ant Killer" and "Bioluminescence"

Pleiades: "The Journey Down"

Quarterly West: "God on the Treadmill"

Sonora Review: "Childhood Incident"

Southwest Review: "Time and Place"

Southern Humanities Review: "Stark Brothers"

Tampa Review: "Adwaitya and the Fruit Fly," "Cocktail Party," and "Had I Been There, Had It Been Me"

West Branch: "Two Apples"

Western Humanities Review: "Beetle Orgy" and "The Colossus at Rhodes"

"Holding Hands" appeared in *Poetic Voices Without Borders*, Robert L. Giron, ed. (Gival Press, 2005).

"Beetle Orgy" was reprinted in *The Pushcart Book of Poetry: The Best Poems from the First 30 Years of the Pushcart Prize*, Joan Murray, ed. (Pushcart Press, 2006), and in *Pushcart Prize 2005: Best of the Small Presses*, Bill Henderson, ed. (Pushcart Press, 2004).

"Time and Place" was reprinted on *Poetry Daily* (www.poems.
com), December 6, 2006, and on *Verse Daily* (www.versedaily.org),
December 20, 2006.

Some of these poems appeared in a chapbook, *The Auctioneer Bangs
His Gavel* (Kent State University Press, 2006).

I am grateful to the Culture Works of Montgomery County, Ohio,
for a 2006 grant that supported the writing of this book.

My deepest thanks to those who offered suggestions and support:
Charles Derry, Cody Enloe, Edward Hirsch, Richard Howard,
Dorianne Laux, Sean Morris, and Alan Michael Parker.

Thanks also to Nathan Pendlebury and Keith Sweeney of National
Museums Liverpool, Lady Lever Art Gallery, for their assistance
with Leighton's painting, and to editor Richard Mathews for his
kindness and diligence.

About the Author

Benjamin S. Grossberg is the winner of the 2008 Tampa Review Prize for Poetry. His first book, *Underwater Lengths in a Single Breath,* won the 2005 Snyder Prize and was published by Ashland Poetry Press in 2007. His poems have appeared widely in literary journals, including *Paris Review, Southwest Review,* and *North American Review.* His awards include a Pushcart Prize as well as arts grants from the Ohio Arts Council, the Cultural Arts Council of Houston and Harris County, and Culture Works of Montgomery County, Ohio. He taught for eight years at Antioch College until its closing in the summer of 2008. He now works as an assistant professor teaching creative writing and poetry at the University of Hartford.

About the Book

Sweet Core Orchard is set in Adobe Garamond Pro types based on the sixteenth century roman types of Claude Garamond and the complementary italic types of Robert Granjon. Titling on the cover and title page is Adobe Trajan Pro, adapted from Frederic Goudy designs inspired by the lettering on the base of the Trajan Column in Rome. The cover and dust jacket were designed by Richard Mathews and Ana Montalvo; the book was designed and typeset by Richard Mathews at the University of Tampa Press. It has been printed on acid-free recycled text paper in support of the Green Press Initiative by Thomson-Shore of Dexter, Michigan.

♟ Poetry from the University of Tampa Press

Jenny Browne, *At Once*

Jenny Browne, *The Second Reason*

Richard Chess, *Chair in the Desert*

Richard Chess, *Tekiah*

Richard Chess, *Third Temple*

Kevin Jeffery Clarke, *The Movie of Us*

Jane Ellen Glasser, *Light Persists**

Benjamin S. Grossberg, *Sweet Core Orchard**

Kathleen Jesme, *Fire Eater*

Steve Kowit, *The First Noble Truth**

Lance Larsen, *In All Their Animal Brilliance**

Julia B. Levine, *Ask**

Julia B. Levine, *Ditch-tender*

Sarah Maclay, *Whore**

Sarah Maclay, *The White Bride*

John Willis Menard, *Lays in Summer Lands*

Barry Silesky, *This Disease*

Jordan Smith, *For Appearances**

Jordan Smith, *The Names of Things Are Leaving*

Lisa M. Steinman, *Carslaw's Sequences*

Marjorie Stelmach, *A History of Disappearance*

Richard Terrill, *Coming Late to Rachmaninoff*

Matt Yurdana, *Public Gestures*

* Denotes winner of the Tampa Review Prize for Poetry